WHY THEY THRIVE

UNDERSTANDING YOUR TEAM'S NATURAL INSTINCTS TO BUILD AN AUTONOMOUS ORGANIZATION

MORGAN R. HUTCHINGS

KOLBE-CERTIFIED CONSULTANT | STRATEGIC COMMUNICATION COACH

Why They Thrive: Understanding Your Team's Natural Instincts to Build an Autonomous Organization by Morgan Hutchings

ISBN 978-1-0733-5533-4

TABLE OF CONTENTS

PREFACE 7

SECTION 1: THE PROBLEMS | 11
MINDSET 15
COMMUNICATION 21
TEAM CULTURE.. 35

SECTION 2: THE CONCEPTS | 39
CONATIVE 45
AFFECTIVE 55
COGNITIVE.. 59

SECTION 3: THE NEXT STEPS | 63
I HAVE A LEADERSHIP TEAM... 67
I NEED A LEADERSHIP TEAM... 71
I'M BURNED OUT. HELP! 75

ABOUT THE AUTHOR 79

FREE RESOURCES 83

TESTIMONIALS 85

Syd, to the moon and back.

Mom, thank you for teaching me to trust my gut,
but listen to my heart.

J&K, for creating this movement,
and leading us to help more people.

PREFACE

My travels have taken me across this great country of The United States of America. I have visited and worked directly with small business owners and entrepreneurs who make up the backbone of the American dream.

Time and time again, my interactions find great visionary entrepreneurs who are exhausted, frustrated, and burnt out with their teams. This pain is real. It is emotionally disturbing for me and, more importantly, to the entrepreneur. This pain is so often the result of a disease I call micro-management. Micro-management is very common amongst entrepreneurs and small-business owners who got where they are today by doing everything and anything needed to get their vision off the ground and turned into a true business. The amount of blood, sweat, and tears these great visionaries have invested in their dream cannot be overlooked but also must be delegated once a start-up begins the transformation to an autonomous organization.

The lack of autonomy amongst team members, which in my experience is most often caused by micro-management, is one of the top-3 drivers of workplace burnout. Just as I cannot imagine leaving my son or daughter in the hands of another person, I can only imagine the angst of leaving your business in the hands of another team member who has true autonomy. I am here to help you, like all of my clients, enjoy the proven path that will allow you to live the lifestyle you desire and build the legacy you have envisioned since you started on this entrepreneurial venture.

If your desire or emotional need to micro-manage or be constantly involved in the day-to-day operations of your business is fueled by a feeling that your team is unable or even unwilling to keep pace with you, I am here to tell you that you are not alone.

The ability to ignite your team to perform at that high-octane level you have had on your journey from startup entrepreneur to millionaire is one experienced by each and every client I have worked with across the world. By using the strategies and tools I will share throughout this book, you will quickly build a strong vision for your growing organization and develop the communication system required to ensure you hire the right people for the right seats on your team and communicate your vision and needs with them properly so that you can turn your entrepreneurial vision into an autonomous organization that produces the lifestyle and legacy you have always wanted.

If you are like many visionary entrepreneurs I have worked with before, you agree with my introduction, and are ready to start implementing the solution immediately. Visit *WhyTheyThrive.com* and complete my questionnaire to get started.

However, if you are anything like me when it comes to problem solving, you most likely need more information, specifics, and detailed testimonials before our journey together will commence...so keep reading!

SECTION 1
THE PROBLEMS

MINDSET

1

MINDSET

THE MOST COMMON PROBLEM I FIND WHEN WORKING WITH A CLI-ent for the first time is a disconnect or breakdown in the mindset between entrepreneur and his/her team.

Many clients voice their frustration over team members that can't keep up, are unwilling to follow instructions or be flexible in their work, or just plain don't have the same level of high-octane commitment to the organization as the founding entrepreneur.

Imagine your business, and your team, in a place where you didn't have to waste mental energy or money on this type of organization stress and could instead focus on the next big thing in your visionary head.

The World Health Organization has named mental burnout and brain fatigue of workplace stress as the health epidemic of the 21st century. The concepts and systems I share in later sections are designed to help you combat workplace stress and the associated health-related costs for individuals and organizations so that you can get back to your vision and building your legacy.

Now, I believe you the visionary entrepreneur have the best intentions in mind when it comes to growing your organization. I also believe that you chose the team around you because you believed they were good people, the right fit, and you wanted them in your orbit. So why then have things suddenly changed and the team you chose seems to be causing more friction, burnout, and energy wasted?

The most common analogy I've found for this phenomenon is 'mission creep' where there has been a shift in objectives or expectations since that team member was chosen by you to join the team. For instance, I have seen a trusted team member who was hired to be a patient care coordinator moved into a phone sales role, and then into a practice management role all within the first year of her employment.

Now I understand the desire to keep good people and trusted team members close to you. This is a must for any growing entrepreneur. However, in this specific example, did the entrepreneur take the time to consider the emotional and psychological impact this would have on his/her team and on the organization as a whole?

Most definitely not.

This inadvertent mistake by nearly all my entrepreneurial clients makes perfect sense when you take a moment to dive deep. As an entrepreneur, you have been a jack-of-all-trades and a master of many of them on your journey from vision to startup and now onto autonomous organization. However, the team members you have brought on board to fill very specific roles, are most often role players for those specific positions where they too can thrive with mastery, autonomy, and purpose; the three key elements to Daniel Pink's motivational theory as outlined in his book *Drive: The Surprising Truth About What Motivates Us.*

Remember, if they had what it takes to be the entrepreneur, jack-of-all-trades and master of many, they most likely would not be on your payroll.

I hope you chose each team member based upon a set of core values, and because they were a good person and right fit for the position *you* chose them for to achieve the vision you shared with your team. If this is the case, your organization most likely does not have a true mindset problem, but rather a communication problem.

COMMUNICATION

COMMUNICATION

POOR COMMUNICATION IN AN ORGANIZATION IS THE SINGLE MOST destructive force I have come across in my journey with entrepreneurs and businesses. The complexity of communication is what holds many entrepreneurs back from fulfilling their vision. With four types of communication, three crucial parts to each communication, and four modifiers to each message, the task for clear communication can be daunting to even those of us with a background and degree in communication. I can't imagine what a visionary who is known for working alone goes through while trying to understand and communicate with a team of individuals.

FOUR COMMUNICATION FORMATS

1. Verbal
2. Non-Verbal
3. Written
4. Visual

THREE CRUCIAL PARTS TO A COMMUNICATION

1. Sender
2. Message
3. Recipient

FOUR MODIFIERS TO EACH MESSAGE

1. Feedback
2. Environment
3. Context
4. Interference

As you can tell, truly understanding the individuals who make up your team and finding a healthy way to communicate with them is key to fulfilling your vision and for avoiding the missed expectations that cause stress, strain, and burnout in your organization.

In my experience working with entrepreneurs across the world as a Kolbe Certified Consultant and Strategic Communication Coach, the most common breakdowns in communication manifest in:

1. Sharing Your Vision
2. Hiring & Onboarding
3. Setting Expectations
4. Accountability
5. Recalibration

Let's start with the first, sharing your vision!

This book is for you if you have ever felt exhausted after a 10+ hour workday, or a 50+ hour work week caused by a racing mind, your head beating against the wall, and hours upon hours of answering questions, managing emails, and worrying about your team leaders, team members, and patients/customers/clients.

You are a warrior though, so you dust yourself off, drink a glass of wine and unwind, say your goodnights to your kids and spouse, and then get back to working on your business so that tomorrow morning you can put a smile on your face and get back to your true passion, changing lives with your product or your service!

While you do this daily ritual, your team members are often clocking out at 4:55pm, in their cars by 5:00pm, and won't think about the business again until 9:05 tomorrow morning. This is where the problems of mindset, and more importantly communication, begin and resentment by the entrepreneur is born.

After reading the words of the last few paragraphs, many of you agree right now, that your team 'just doesn't understand.' Actually, you're right! But, in nearly all of my experience working with both small and large organizations the reason is the visionary entrepreneur failed to properly communicate the vision in a way that would be understood by their team members.

For those that like to take quick action, I highly recommend you and your team read *Start With Why* by Simon Sinek. If your team has visual learners, there is a great TED Talk by Simon on YouTube that gets the point across as well. This book is foundational to the work we will do together when we begin solving the mindset, communication, and poisonous team members that are holding you back from your entrepreneurial legacy. In fact, its one of the 48 books that make up the book-of-the-month portion of my team development and level up program.

One of the most frequent questions I receive when speaking to groups of entrepreneurs, owners, and managers about becoming better communicators of their vision is, "shouldn't my team just do what I tell them because its their job and I'm their boss?"

The short answer is, yes. The longer answer is rooted in human psychology and motivation. If you remember earlier in the book, I mentioned Daniel Pink's theory and how team members work for mastery, autonomy, and purpose. My job as your coach is to help you build an 'autonomous organization' of thriving members who help you realize your vision. Here is what my experience working with thousands of individuals, hundreds of new hires, and business owners around the world has proven time and time again; your current team needs to know your vision; your why or your purpose! Later in the book we will discuss the proven process for doing so.

The second most common breakdown in communication occurs during the hiring and onboarding process; or should I say lack thereof.

Time and time again, I've seen entrepreneurs and business owners hire based upon emotion or feeling, this is called using the affective part of the mind. This part of the mind will often change, and then the new team member is quickly viewed as not such a good hire after all.

The number one reason I see this hiring mistake is the organization lacks a written hiring process developed around the conative (instinctual) and cognitive needs of the position in question. This type of system would include job position posts, job descriptions, core values fit assessment, five core roles and responsibilities of the position, and a proven interview and selection process based upon objective measures, level of mindset, natural instincts for the position, and expectations of the supervisor or entrepreneur. Remember, the process and systems I will share with you are built to help you lead a thriving and autonomous organization that contributes to your vision and legacy.

This topic is one that is closest to my heart, as I've watched countless team members, including myself, be hired as the next great superstar, quickly beaten up by the entrepreneur or organization, and then let go as a no-good performer. Not only is this lack of upfront communication to new hires unfair, but it also brings disruption to an organization, and makes our fellow humans feel broken and unworthy. This is suffering that could easily have been avoided by properly communicating the 'why' for the new hire and the specific hiring process for the position to everyone upfront.

Once a candidate is selected, the hiring process becomes the onboarding process. This too requires intentional communication with all stakeholders involved to ensure your new addition to the team is setup for success in his or her role and can begin contributing to your team.

Breakdowns in this area often involve not communicating with the new hire regarding what they should know prior to orientation day, what the training schedule looks like, how long they will be in training, and how they will be held accountable to learning core responsibilities, what their assigned data points are, what 90-day projects they are responsible for, and how they go about learning the required daily, weekly, and monthly tasks that round out their role.

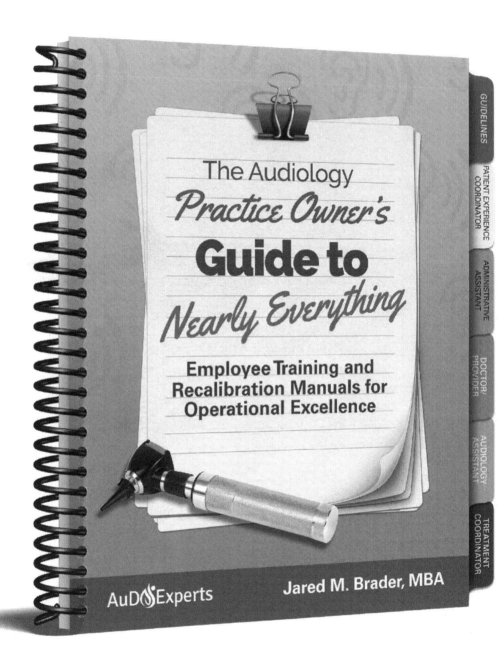

In addition to good communication with the new hire, does your organization have a communicated process for the onboarding of new team members so that they have everything they need on day one? Items such as name badges, uniforms, parking passes, office space, telephones, computers and any other tools or equipment an employee needs should be setup and ready to go on the very first day.

I've seen countless organizations who do a great job during the new team member onboarding, only to have left their current team in the dark. This causes a level of chaos, uncertainty, and stress on the current team members anytime the entrepreneur wishes to grow the team and bring on new team members.

If you've made it through the first two most common areas of communication breakdown without thinking to yourself that your organization needs to have me complete a practice assessment, then congratulations and I applaud you for your communication savvy.

The next most common area of communication breakdown I find during practice/business assessments is the area of team member expectations. Now I probably have some of you cheering at the thought that we are going to outline and hold the team accountable to certain communicated expectations. As your coach, I'm also going to hold you the entrepreneur and business owner to certain expectations as well.

Let's start with your current communication strategy for team expectations. Do you have a place where data is tracked, shared by all, and discussed weekly? What is your current feedback loop for when expectations are not met weekly? Does your process of identification, discussion, and solving expectation concerns include both verbal and written communication? Do you or your team leaders have quarterly organizational checkups, have non-formal quarterly conversations, and incentivize your team for bringing issues, challenges, and ideas to the group as a whole?

As you take a moment to think through the complexity of communicated expectations, and the natural feedback loop needed for progress, I'll leave you with one additional question. *Have you spoken the unspoken expectations in a way that your team can hear and understand?*

Here's something you can implement at your next weekly meeting. Take a look around your organization and see if you have any unspoken rules or expectations. If you have ever said, "Well they just know that is what I want" then you have an unspoken expectation that needs to be stated out loud, written down, and made known!

Now, let's discuss the expectations on you the entrepreneur or business owner. If I was to interview your team members today, and asked, *"What expectations of your boss/entrepreneur/employer do you have?"* would they be able to answer uniformly?

"EMPLOYEES WHO BELIEVE THAT MANAGEMENT IS **CONCERNED ABOUT THEM AS A WHOLE PERSON**—NOT JUST AN EMPLOYEE—ARE MORE PRODUCTIVE, MORE SATISFIED, MORE FULFILLED. SATISFIED EMPLOYEES MEAN SATISFIED CUSTOMERS, WHICH LEADS TO PROFITABILITY."

ANNE M. MULCAHY

The goal of any great leader should not be to pay employees, create jobs, or followers, it should be to create more leaders! Do you commit and execute on providing your team members the tools, training, and support to master their role? Do you provide the freedom and decision-making capacity for your team to be autonomous in their daily responsibilities? Is your team aligned with and invited to participate in a significant way toward your greater purpose?

You've probably heard the famous Richard Branson quote from 2014, "*Train people well enough that they can leave, treat them well enough so they don't want to.*" When deciding on how your organization will implement this quote, consider training opportunities like the Disney Institute, the Ritz Carlton Leadership Center, Tony Robbins' Unleash the Power Within, and other life-improving investments for your team.

Creating a healthy, two-way dialogue with your team members and their direct reports will be crucial to building an autonomous team with spoken expectations that contribute to your vision and legacy.

At this point in the book, you are probably noticing that communication (verbal, non-verbal, written, and visual) is the key element in most organizational problems. You have now seen how communicating your vision, your hiring/onboarding, and your expectations are foundational to the development of an autonomous organization.

Beyond the upfront communication of the aforementioned areas, the next two areas of communication breakdown are *accountability* and *recalibration* which require ongoing communication from team leaders who are *not* the entrepreneur.

In my work with clients a common theme has shown up, visionary entrepreneurs tend to be bored and frustrated by the need to communicate accountability. Which makes sense as the entrepreneur's key roles are visionary, culture, and big picture ideas. Your next question might be, "Then who communicates accountability in the organization?"

Great question! The short answer is everyone. The longer answer involves a system of accountability and a culture of accountability, both of which we dive deep on in the coming pages of this book.

When communicating accountability, I often ask my clients if their individual team members have specific numbers for which they are held accountable. If so, are those numbers being achieved weekly, how is the organization trending over the last thirty or ninety days, and what is actively being done by the team member and the organization to make sure that number is achieved?

Does your organization currently have systems in place to hold team members accountable to your vision? How soon does data flow up from the front lines to your team leaders and onto you?

Many of my clients are stuck on the topic of accountability because they lack written processes and how-to guides for each step in their core business functions. By lacking a written process, your organization cannot hold its team accountable to anything specific besides results. This might sound okay to you now, but results are outcomes based upon actions or processes and results are lagging indicators, meaning by the time the result is published it is too late to make a difference. However, if you hold your team accountable to following a specific process, or completing certain tasks, you will be able to alter the outcomes on a more consistent basis.

I'M A FIRM BELIEVER THAT **WITHOUT ACCOUNTABILITY,**
THE BUSINESS IS COMPLETE CHAOS.

What if McDonald's didn't hold its team accountable to the steps and order in which they've determined a Big Mac is made? Their Big Macs would be inconsistent, and their customers would lose trust in what a Big Mac is, and over-time McDonalds would lose its value proposition.

I'll leave you with this question, does your business have a written process and expected outcome for the way in which it does business at each core function so that your team leaders, team members, and culture can be held accountable?

The fifth most common area of communication breakdown I find in organizations is recalibration. You see, many people use 'accountability' to identify who should be promoted or let go. But, in fact, having healthy communication in accountability leads to proper communication in the recalibration area.

In your organization, do you have a written recalibration plan for team members in each role? When you or your team leaders notice accountability slipping, results not meeting expectations, or team members losing focus on the vision you have as an entrepreneur, what do you do next? Have you communicated to your team the steps to getting back on track?

In any organization, professional sports team, symphony orchestra, or team of individuals for that matter, there will come a time when someone or something is off track. These moments are points of inflection for the team, either the individual will begin a recalibration plan and work their way back into contributing to your vision, or they won't. As long as your organization has a recalibration plan communicated in writing, demonstrated visually, and supported verbally you will continue to quickly address any issues that arise within your organization. However, without a strong recalibration plan, your organization may continue to burn employees out, have increasing drama amongst team members, and be unable to achieve your vision.

You might think you can skip the recalibration plan and just replace the struggling individuals, but I'm here to tell you that this is only a short-term solution that will be inadequate. If you've replaced a team member only to find the next one struggling in one of the five most common areas of communication breakdown I've just outlined, then you may have a team culture problem.

"IF YOU JUST COMMUNICATE, YOU CAN GET BY.
BUT IF YOU **COMMUNICATE SKILLFULLY**, YOU CAN **WORK MIRACLES**."

JIM ROHN

TEAM CULTURE

TEAM CULTURE

I WOULD IMAGINE AFTER READING THE FIRST TWO SECTIONS ON mindset and communication problems your mind is racing with all the little things that are holding you back on your entrepreneurial quest. From the exhaustion, frustration, and burnout you feel each week, to the micro-management that is necessary to get your unable or unwilling team to keep pace with your high-octane speed, you are ready to begin working smarter not harder in the next phase of your vision.

After mindset and communication problems, the third most common problem that I help clients improve is their team culture. **Do not underestimate the importance of building a great team culture in today's workplace.** My research for this book led me to great corporations, visionary leaders, all-star athletes, human instincts, and world-class business systems, and that research all pointed back to one common theme: *team culture!*

As you analyze the team you have put together to help you achieve your entrepreneurial vision, are they truly rallied around and consistently communicating their contribution to the greater purpose of the organization? As a team that takes ownership of their contribution and how they work together, they will have a strong shared vision and will continuously search for ways to improve.

Remember, your team cannot simply be forced to be a team; they need a desire to belong and contribute. The most important job of any entrepreneur is to clearly articulate your vision and how the team will achieve it. The members of the team need to understand how their contribution fits into the bigger picture.

Reinforcing the bigger vision of the team is something to be continually bolstered. It cannot be said once, or posted on a wall in the break room, and then forgotten; leaders need to find ways to infuse this sense of purpose on an ongoing basis for the continued growth and productivity of the team.

Now that I mention 'leaders,' you and your organization must emphasize mentorship over management. Fostering a culture of leading from within will play an important role in team culture.

Consider this, have you invested in teaching your team the benefits of constructive feedback that encourages productivity rather than shame or embarrassment? Have you set aside one of your monthly full-day trainings to teach the concept of healthy friction? Does your organization have a system for team member feedback, q/a, or innovation to instill a culture that everyone has something to offer and contribute?

On this topic, how well do you know your team members and their unique strengths, weaknesses, and skills yet to be developed? Remember, a great leader learns to draw out the talent around them not simply use the people like a resource. Are you currently taking the opportunity to celebrate birthdays, achievements, and holidays with your team? Does your monthly team awesomeness report cover all the amazingness of your team both inside and outside their work life?

One of my favorite concepts in building a team culture is that of providing feedback. This is one of the most common areas where entrepreneurs mistakenly foster a _negative team culture._

In observing business environments around the country, I often notice entrepreneurs who only provide feedback when something goes wrong, did not hit the mark, or is off track. This feedback loop does harm to the team culture by instilling fear, doubt, and failure into the team. Instead of waiting until a problem occurs to give feedback, try developing a habit of regular feedback, both by catching your team doing something right, and with quick reprimands when something is done wrong. My favorite book for helping you and your team leaders build a great culture is _The One Minute Manager_ by Ken Blanchard and Spencer Johnson.

If your team culture is not growing, it is most likely dying. Do you or your organization promote and foster a culture of learning where every person is encouraged to continue expanding their skill sets? Do you provide access to ongoing training and personal development programs like Tony Robbins, John Maxwell, The Disney Institute, Ritz Carlton Leadership, and for my audiology clients the _www.ELAuniversity.com_?

The expansion of online learning throughout the global pandemic of 2020 has made it easier to help your team grow, achieve, and thrive both personally and professionally as they can now learn on their own time, in their own way.

Our greatest job as leaders is to develop more leaders. Encourage your team to continue learning by offering book of the month bonus opportunities, level-up programs, personal development courses, and rewards for goal achievement. These strategies will prevent your team from becoming complacent, stagnant, or bored in their positions.

Development of team culture by incorporating the strategies and recommendations from the first section of this book will allow your team to learn new skills, be engaged, and add value to your team and workplace.

"LIFE'S PERSISTENT AND MOST URGENT QUESTION IS 'WHAT ARE YOU DOING FOR OTHERS?'"

MARTIN LUTHER KING JR.

Now, I'd like to dive into the concepts of cognitive, conative, and affective parts of the mind so that you will have the knowledge and tools to be a better leader, communicator, and entrepreneur as you seek to fulfill your vision.

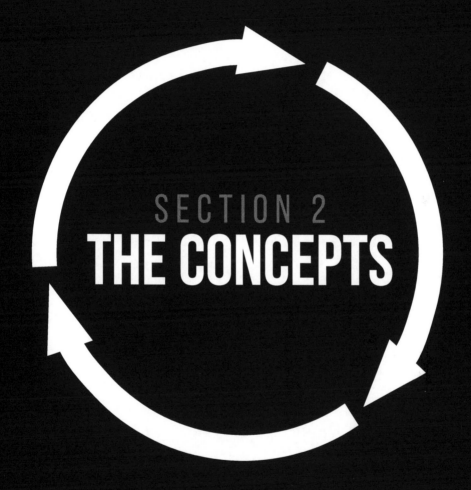

SECTION 2
THE CONCEPTS

IF YOU ARE STILL WITH ME AT THIS POINT IN THE BOOK, IT'S most likely that you've experienced these same problems within your organization, and you have decided you do not want to repeat the mistakes of the past. Congratulations on your desire to learn more about the three parts of the mind and how a better understanding of them will enable you to build an autonomous organization that is ready, willing, and able to help you fulfill your vision and legacy.

In my journey to help entrepreneurs like you understand why some team members thrive and others don't, my research has led me to become a better student of human behavior and psychology. In the coming pages of this section, I'll lay out the core concepts that play an integral role in developing a team with reduced stress, strain, and tension.

To begin, I'd like to share the three parts of the human mind: conative, affective, and cognitive. Simply, the doing part, the feeling part, and the thinking part. They work together to make your team members productive.

As a Kolbe Certified Consultant, and student of human behavior and communication, I've found the greatest gains in team development by focusing on the conative part of the mind. This area is the 'how' an individual works. This part of the mind is not new; in fact, Aristotle and Socrates both recognized its existence in the fourth century BC. However, it wasn't until 1987 when Kathy Kolbe created the Kolbe Index to measure human action. She said, "Instincts on their own are a subconscious force and cannot be measured, but we can measure the actions we see, observe, and report."

After I dive into the *why*, *how*, and *what* regarding the conative part of the mind, I will also share with you the other two parts of the mind. Both parts have assessments and tools that are critical to truly understanding your team and helping them thrive in the modern workplace.

— **SYNERGY** —

"THE COMBINED **POWER OF A GROUP** OF THINGS,
WHEN THEY ARE **WORKING TOGETHER**, WHICH IS GREATER THAN
THE TOTAL POWER ACHIEVED BY EACH WORKING SEPARATELY"

THREE PARTS OF THE MIND*

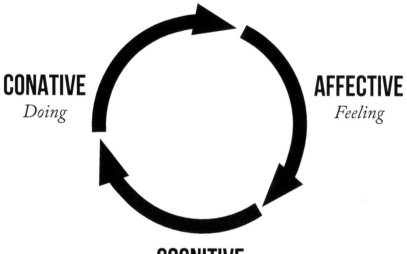

CONATIVE
Doing

AFFECTIVE
Feeling

COGNITIVE
Thinking

CONATIVE *Doing*	**AFFECTIVE** *Feeling*	**COGNITIVE** *Thinking*
Drive	Desires	IQ
Instinct	Motivation	Skills
Necessity	Attitudes	Reason
Mental Energy	Preferences	Knowledge
Innate Force	Emotions	Experience
Talents	Values	Education

*Diagram based on original concept by Kathy Kolbe and Kolbe Corp.

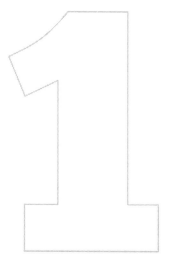

CONATIVE

DESCRIBED IN THE MERRIAM-WEBSTER DICTIONARY AS THE NOUN of "conation: an inclination (such as an instinct, a drive, a wish, or a crazing) to act purposefully" was first used in 1837.

Fast forward 150 years and Kathy Kolbe created the Kolbe Index™ to measure human action. To date, she has created the only validated conative assessment. I've personally seen companies ranging from Fortune 500 to small entrepreneurial organizations rely on the Kolbe Concept™ to accurately predict how team members will get things done within the organization.

Only Kolbe measures the part of the mind that predicts how your people act. The Proven Kolbe System™ will help you be more productive, less stressed, and build teams that get the job done exactly how you need it to fulfill your vision and leave your legacy.

At its core, the theory classifies all human actions into four Conative Action Modes®. Each action mode is divided into three equally powerful zones of operation. Each of your team members operate most effectively in a single zone in the *Fact Finder, Follow Thru, Quick Start,* and *Implementor* modes.

THE FOUR KOLBE ACTION MODES® ARE DEFINED AS:

Fact Finder   how one gathers and shares information

Follow Thru   how one organizes and systematizes

Quick Start   how one deals with risk and uncertainty

Implementor   how one handles space and tangibles

An individual's most effective, instinctive methods of acting are measurable, and do not change over time. These results are not biased by gender, age or race. In addition, the reliability and consistency of one's action mode has been proven in a fifteen-year test/re-test study out of Arizona State University.

When you and I begin working together, or if you take advantage of the free resources at the back of this book, our starting point will be understanding the most foundational assessment of the Kolbe Concept®. This self-assessment is the Kolbe A™ Index. With this simple assessment, we can identify your conative architecture to give you guidance that suits your Action Modes®.

Your Kolbe A™ result will be a perfect score. In fact, they all are. Your conative attributes define the way *you* act (take action) and *your* approach to productivity. Understanding your unique attributes as strengths and leverage them to do more, more naturally, in every aspect of your daily life.

Deploying this assessment throughout your business you will begin to understand that each team member has his or her own performance sweet spot—a mode of operation (MO) in which he or she excels—that drives success when focused on the right tasks.

This conative assessment tends to help both individuals and teams execute at higher levels, and could answer questions like:

How can I tell if I have the right people in the right roles based on the tasks required by the job?

I hired somebody who is very smart and motivated, why aren't they more productive and reaching their potential?

How do these team members handle various methods of problem solving? For example, how will they deal with risk and uncertainty? Are they going to follow our established processes or find shortcuts?

MORGAN HUTCHINGS
Kolbe A™ Index Result

CONGRATULATIONS MORGAN
You Got a Perfect Score on the Kolbe A™ Index

You are fantastic at making comparisons, documenting information, and defining priorities. You can be counted on to research historical details, become an expert in areas of special interest, and make strategic decisions.

Kolbe Action Modes®

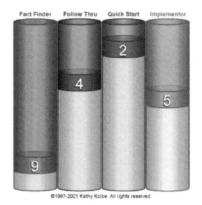

How do we know this? You told us when you completed the Kolbe A™ Index. Our proprietary algorithm sorted out your answers and came up with the pattern of your MO (Modus Operandi).

Your Kolbe result is so individualized, only 5% of the population is likely to have one just like it.

"When I took the Kolbe A™ Index I finally understood who I was. Years of always feeling like I never had enough information from those around me. Once I discovered the power of my initiating action mode 'Fact Finder' and zone of 'Specify' I changed my communication strategy and gave myself permission to ask the right questions, in the right way, to feel fulfilled in my career path."

—Morgan Hutchings

To the left, you can see my actual Kolbe A™ Index result. I'm an initiating fact finder with the _need_, not desire or want, to have as much information and specific details as possible before moving on. That's also why I'm sick at the thought of releasing this book with anything less than 2,500 pages and as many details as my instincts believe are needed to effectively convey the entirety of my conative knowledge.

If you decide to work with me to reduce team member stress, strain, and tension within your organization, I will dive into the 18-page Kolbe A™ Index with each of your team members for a thorough interpretation. This initial conversation will last about an hour and help your team members begin the process of aligning who they are with what your vision requires of them. For more examples, your own Kolbe A™ Index and a complete sample report, visit **WhyTheyThrive.com** and request your free resources!

My specific result explains so much about why I was never the entrepreneur, but rather the chief strategist to top-producing entrepreneurs, business owners, and risk-taking individuals.

When I am truly free to solve problems my way, here is how I will go about it based upon my natural instincts:

1. I'll start the problem-solving process by fact checking and determining practical and appropriate priorities.
2. Next, I check the strength and durability of available materials.
3. Then, I look for ways to fit the project into the system.
4. Finally, I advocate for what needs to stay the same.

As you can see, the order in which I expend my energy, is in most cases fundamentally different than your entrepreneurial way of fire, aim, ready! That's not to say your way or my way is better, but rather we are both perfect in our modes of operation and would be complementary and synergistic to one another when building an autonomous organization.

Assessing and understanding the instinctive methods of all of your team members will create a less stressful work environment where your team is more satisfied and more productive in their positions. I look forward to working with you and your team on this element of organizational development.

About this point in my coaching, an entrepreneurial client is ready to ask, *"Great Morgan. So, now I know my team's Kolbe A™ Index, but how do I get them to start helping me get shit done?"*

Great question!

For purposes of explaining what's next in the conative realm, I will assume either you have no communication problems in your organization, or that you and I have worked together with your team to overcome those before getting to the Kolbe B™ and Kolbe C™ Index.

These indexes are two additional tools to help increase your employees' performance capabilities and better align expectations and requirements for a specific job. These indexes, when compared to the Kolbe A, measure the gaps within your organization. They help you solve problems and provide solutions for emerging issues. The Kolbe B Index measures the employee's own expectations about fulfilling his/her job. A significant difference between the expectations in the Kolbe B and the reality of the Kolbe A identifies a stress point or strain. The Kolbe C Index measures the supervisor's requirements for the individual's job. A significant difference between the requirements in the Kolbe C and the reality of the Kolbe A identifies another point of stress or tension. An individual attempting to work against his or her grain—whether because of perceived expectations or real requirements—needs additional coaching.

After we have a complete profile of your team, their perception of their role, and your own requirements of the role we can work together with a series of **Leadership Reports™** and **Organizational Analysis™** tools, which I have access to as a Kolbe Certified Consultant, to maximize the effectiveness of your team. These reports assess team synergy and effectiveness and identify areas of individual and team stress in the organization. Some of the tools include:

SPREADSHEET OF STRENGTHS™

Spreadsheet of Strengths is an at-a-glance reference of the organization's available talent. It lists all of your team members and their Kolbe results.

TEAM SYNERGY REPORT™

Synergy results from instinctive diversity. Groups with optimal synergy have proven as much as 225% more productive!

INERTIA ANALYSIS™

Just as inertia in the physical world inhibits forward momentum, mental inertia bogs down a team's efforts. The Inertia Analysis will identify reduced productivity causes by evaluating the amount of energy within Action Modes.

LEADERSHIP BOTTOM LINE™

This report predicts the team's viability and projects its probability of success.

My heart truly is having palpitations right now, as I just went so far against my natural instincts by laying out an entire advanced certification in conation using bullet points and one-line summaries... *definitely causing my own conative stress right now!*

Before I get ahead of myself, you may be ready to ask; *"This sounds great for my current team, but how does it apply to my organization as we grow and hire new team members?"*

As I'm sure you are aware, selecting job candidates who have the highest potential for success can be a challenging task, even more so in today's post-pandemic work-remotely environment. By defining the instinctive requirements for the position up-front, you can objectively determine what type of person will succeed.

For best practices, before hiring a new team member, you should complete a Kolbe RightFit™ for the position. This assists in the selection, placement, and retention process, ensuring that people who are hired add value and do not detract from the synergy already in place within your organization. It facilitates making an informed decision regarding the appropriateness of a job candidate's natural abilities for the requirements of a specific job, without bias by gender, age, or race, according to EEOC standards.

Kolbe RightFit™ measures the methods of problem-solving the position requires and defines the innate problem solving behaviors with which an individual applicant will succeed. When a person's instinctive approach to problem solving meshes with the demands of a job, he/she will work more productively and more successfully for your organization and vision.

In my years of experiences working with entrepreneurial owners, Inc. 500/5000 business owners, and the front-line team members of organizations around the world on a topic that most, if not all of you, have never heard of in the traditional human behavior and psychology materials, I can make one guarantee to you...your team has untapped potential waiting to be harnessed to fulfill your vision and build that legacy.

"TWO THINGS CONTROL MEN'S NATURE— INSTINCT AND EXPERIENCE."

BLAISE PASCAL

AFFECTIVE

THE AFFECTIVE PART OF THE MIND IS THE ONE THAT MOST OF you are probably familiar with. Affective is best simplified to 'feeling' or 'emotion.' A person's affective strengths lie in their ability to use emotion effectively.

Most of the popular personal assessments on the market are measuring the affective part of the mind. This type of assessment is useful for understanding what motivates your team, knowing what their values are, and how they prefer to interact with others.

If you're having issues on a team with one or two specific individuals and you think it's driven by a clash of values or what each person views as important, or how they prefer to interact, you may use one of the many affective assessments on the market such as Clifton-Strengths® assessment, or Predictive Index® or even DiSC®, Myers-Briggs, and Enneagram. While these assessments are great for spotting differences in values or interpersonal skills in terms of reliability and validity within the psychological community, they often come up short because a person's likes, dislikes, preferences, and even motivations will change over time.

Affective assessments tend to help individuals understand their own motivations, and may answer questions like:

How can I tell if this person enjoys working with others or prefers working alone?

Is this person motivated by external praise and team success, or by their own internal drive to succeed?

Do this person's values (honesty, fairness, and responsibility) align with the company and job?

The Myers-Briggs Type Indicator measures a person's reaction to circumstances and assigns a 'personality type' that defines the emotional tools that the assessment taker uses to cope, grow, and communicate in their daily life.

Remember, affective assessment results may change over time, and I would not recommend building an entire entrepreneurial team or system around any of them in particular. Through my 'boots-on-the-ground' learning, interacting with thousands of individuals in organizations both large and small, the best advice I can give when it comes to this area is to always assume best intentions on the part of your team members.

The most impactful affective assessment I use with clients and their teams is the CliftonStrengths® assessment developed by Donald O. Clifton in 1999. Clifton would later be recognized by the

American Psychological Association as "the father of strengths-based psychology and the grandfather of positive psychology". You can read more in *StrengthsFinder 2.0*, which is among Amazon's Top-20 best-selling books of all time.

This affective self-assessment consists of 177 questions that will help determine the true you. It measures talents—the natural pattern of thinking, feeling, and behaving of an individual—and categorizes them into 34 CliftonStrengths® themes.

Gaining a true understanding of each team member's conative, affective, and cognitive minds will allow you to be a better leader and develop systems in which your team can succeed.

By developing a strengths-based culture you will be setting your organization up for real organic growth that fulfills your vision.

The organizations I've worked with to create a strengths-based culture succeed because:

- They engage their employees.

- They surround team members with leaders who coach them to maximize their potential.

- They provide an exceptional team member experience and specific level-up opportunities.

Based upon what I've seen within entrepreneurial organizations, it was no surprise when I learned that organizations with a strengths-based culture experience higher employee engagement, retention, productivity and performance. **Talk about creating an autonomous organization!**

Here are a few specific data points directly from CliftonStrengths®
website regarding their internal tracking results for organizations that
have deployed strengths-based development:

- 29% increased profit

- 19% increased sales

- 72% lower attrition

- 7% higher customer engagement

Those are some impressive statistics, and they directly relate to building an autonomous organization that is ready-willing-and-able to
fulfill your entrepreneurial vision and help you establish the legacy
you desire to leave.

Next, in the following image I'd like to share my Top-5 Clifton-
Strengths® with you, and then using my experience with a strengths-
based culture outline human behaviors that would be expected from
someone with my strengths when they are operating from a healthy
mindset and also the behaviors to spot when operating from an un-
healthy or stressed state of mind within the organization.

Morgan's CliftonStrengths® Top-5
Focus on Strengthening

1. **Significance**

2. **Futuristic**

3. **Strategic**

4. **Responsibility**

5. **Activator**

COGNITIVE

THE THIRD PART OF THE MIND IS COGNITIVE. COGNITIVE ASSESS-
ments evaluate your knowledge and skills—how smart a team member is and what they know. One of the top generic cognitive ability assessments is the Wonderlic Cognitive Ability Test, which is used to help you understand what your team members know of their general ability to reason. These assessments are rarely used in group or team settings, but individually could help leadership determine where their team needs additional training.

Now, depending on your specific niche, cognitive assessments may vary. For example, in audiology and hearing healthcare the cognitive assessments used might be national board-certification, the International Licensing Exam, or assessments found on a training platform like *www.ELAuniversity.com*

In other niches, examples of a cognitive assessment might be the state bar exam, a certified financial planner exam, or dental/medical/chiropractor exams.

Simply put, cognitive ability describes a candidate's ability to learn, adapt, solve problems, and understand relevant instructions. The single-best predictor of specific job performance, a cognitive ability test helps you understand if a candidate can do the job.

Remember, there are three parts of the mind and the human behavior and psychology that goes into bringing those aspects together gives a more complete picture than cognitive ability alone. The reality is that some of the brightest people don't always get a lot done and hiring a team of super-smart people doesn't mean your team will function well. Great leaders will consider all three parts of the mind when developing an autonomous organization and leading their team members.

Inside your organization, and throughout your hiring, onboarding, and introductory period for new team members you should have in place cognitive assessments that make sure your team is prepared with the knowledge and reasoning needed to complete their five core responsibilities. If you have a team member that does not pass, or struggles, this could be a great early warning indicator that recalibration is needed before the problem becomes systemic and you're ready to free their future (fire them)!

"THE BEST TIP FOR BUSINESS OWNERS—
HIRE SLOW, FIRE FAST."

PAUL FOSTER

THREE PARTS OF THE MIND*

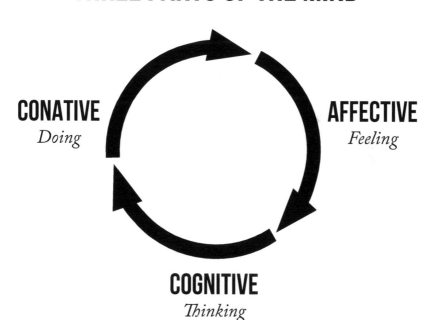

CONATIVE
Doing

AFFECTIVE
Feeling

COGNITIVE
Thinking

SECTION 3

THE NEXT STEPS

SCHEDULE A
FREE 'WHY THEY THRIVE'
STRATEGY SESSION

TalkToMorgan.com

THE NEXT STEPS

CONGRATULATIONS, AND MY APOLOGIES! YOU'VE MADE IT through the heartburn of reliving your frustration and burnout over the last two sections.

I suspect you are still with me at this point in the book because my boots-on-the-ground experiences training organizations align with what you are facing as you work to turn your visionary dream into an autonomous organization.

In the coming pages I will lay out the exact next steps I have used time and again with both small organizations and Inc. 500/5000 recognized companies to turn dreams into reality for entrepreneurs wanting more.

As we begin our journey working together, keep in mind my role as your coach is to help you work smarter, not harder, to understand yourself and your team's natural instincts; hire the right people for the right positions, build and deploy a million-dollar communication structure; avoid burnout and turnover on your team; and understand when to 'free the future' of someone on your team.

In the coming pages, I will outline the three most common starting points where clients and I begin, what the main theme of those areas are, and how to take the next step to gain traction in your organization.

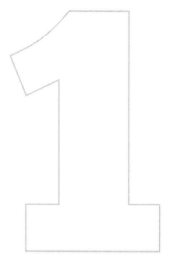

I HAVE A
LEADERSHIP TEAM.

THE MOST COMMON VISIONARY ENTREPRENEUR WHO ENGAGES me for coaching and advice begins our relationship by informing me that they already have a few 'go-to' trusted team members.

This entrepreneur has had success getting from vision to where they are now, but they are starting to feel the pressure increase and the weight of the day-to-day business slowing them down from the next great leap forward.

The trusted 'go-to' team members have most often been by the entrepreneur's side from early on, often with an intense commitment to the visionary personally and willingness to do anything to help.

These team members are often great workers, sometimes even decent managers, but their relationship with the visionary entrepreneur is keeping them from being true autonomous leaders within your organization.

The most common reason is due to their closeness to the visionary entrepreneur who will always hold more intrinsic leadership than the team member. As John Maxwell once put it, *"Leadership is influence, nothing more nothing less. Whoever has the most influence in the room has the leadership."*

As loyal servants, these 'go-to' team members have built their careers as your task manager, your doer, or subordinate. If you are like most of my clients, you probably feel as though you owe them a leadership position, or they have earned it through years of service. Chances are high you will be unable to mentor them into autonomous leaders.

You've probably increased their compensation over the years and find yourself getting less production or return on the investment in each passing year.

Common thoughts about these trusted team members are:

- *I feel like I'm micro-managing them.*
- *They can't keep up with what I'm trying to do.*
- *They don't seem to understand my vision.*
- *They feel like I'm always changing.*

If any of this sounds familiar to you, and you are adamant that you are willing and able to mentor these trusted team members into leaders, then we must work together to:

1. Understand their natural instincts.
2. Verify they are in the right seat on your team.
3. Make your vision crystal clear.
4. Determine rock solid core values.
5. Set clear expectations for the week, month, quarter, year, three-year, and 10-year vision of your organization.
6. Assign these team members five core responsibilities.
7. Finally, and most importantly, you must be willing to give them complete and unilateral autonomy in their role and responsibilities.

That's right! This group of trusted team members is most likely not fulfilling your leadership needs due to their lack of autonomy within the organization.

A startup organization was built upon the blood, sweat, and tears of the visionary entrepreneur and to become an autonomous organization, team members must be empowered to be self-starters, giving them stewardship over their work and their environment, and providing them support rather than exerting control.

The benefits of promoting autonomy include increased feelings of ownership and loyalty, improved productivity and reduce overhead costs, and higher job satisfaction.

If you already have a leadership team, and you're ready to take the next step toward an autonomous organization, **schedule a FREE 'Why They Thrive' Consultation by visiting** *TalkToMorgan.com.*

I NEED A
LEADERSHIP TEAM.

THE SECOND MOST COMMON TYPE OF ENTREPRENEUR THAT reaches out to me is looking for advice on getting their organization ready to make the next big leap forward. In private practice healthcare, this is often hitting two million dollars in revenue.

This visionary wants more out of their organization, knows how hard it was to shoulder the load to this point, and is ready to scale it with a solid leadership team!

Preparing to scale your organization can take time. I've watched some great companies take years to build, train, and implement the proper teams and systems so that when they were ready for their next great period of growth they didn't crumble.

Helping clients envision, and build, a leadership team from the ground up is very rewarding. The process of truly understanding the organization's current state, hearing the vision for the future, and then setting a deadline, responsible parties, and a method of measurement for implementation is as strategic as it gets. If you remember from earlier in the book, Kathy Kolbe describes my mode of operation as 'Strategist!'

If you are the next great visionary entrepreneur who is looking to finally build their leadership dream team to scale their organization to the next level, then I suggest you **schedule a FREE 'Why They Thrive' Strategy Session by visiting** *TalkToMorgan.com* **or scanning the QR code below.**

Our starting point will be a five-step process consisting of:

1. Current State of the Organization
2. Future State of the Organization
3. Timeline for Deployment
4. Who is Responsible for What?
5. How Will We Measure Successful Implementation?

After we've outlined our strategy, we will incorporate my proven hiring, onboarding, and training blueprints to make sure your new team leaders have mastery in their roles and responsibilities in building your autonomous organization.

These programs, in the order and way I use them, have been in development, testing, and proven since 2017 and include:

- Automated Hiring Systems
- Structured Interview Process
- Dynamynd®: Kolbe Decision Ladder for:
  - Individuals, Teams, Culture, Leadership
- Hiring
- Onboarding
- Training
- Recalibration

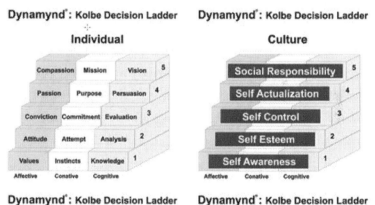

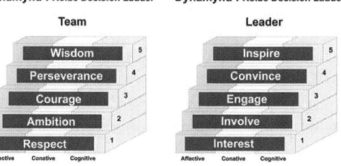

I'M BURNED OUT.
HELP!

THE THIRD, AND MOST FRIGHTENING, TYPE OF ENTREPRENEUR who seems to find their way to my coaching programs and tools is the burnt-out entrepreneur that has nothing left in their emotional bank account. I remember the first such entrepreneur I met, a nice lady from Colorado with seven locations who said, *"I have no shits left to give!"* when I was completing an assessment of her organizational issues.

How frightening!

While I've been around enough entrepreneurs to know that an organization without team leaders may seem like a roller coaster, I just can't imagine how bad it must be to feel helpless, hopeless, and ready to give up on your creation.

Let's consider the impact of the burnt-out entrepreneur on the American economy where those same entrepreneurs are responsible for creating roughly 66% of new jobs and delivering 43% of the United States' gross domestic product.

You, my friend, are a creator and without your contributions, this world, this economy, and your customers/clients/donors would be worse off. With that said, I understand that your tears of frustration and your fears of the never-ending fight is real to you; but I can attest to helping other entrepreneurs such as yourself get back to their purpose, to reconnect with their love, and to focus on their next level-up or new business venture.

If you're the entrepreneur wrestling with doubt or fears of "is all of this worth it," please reach out and **schedule an hour of time with me for a FREE 'Why They Thrive' Consultation by scanning the QR code below or visiting** *TalkToMorgan.com.*

After assessing the current state of your organization and your mindset, I'll be able to help you:

- recenter your organization around your greater purpose or calling in life

- build an autonomous organization, freeing you of the day-to-day stressors

- create more time for your family, friends, and relationships of importance

- give you the freedom and independence of owning a business rather than holding a high paying J.O.B.

ABOUT THE AUTHOR

Morgan R. Hutchings, a Kolbe Certified Consultant and Strategic Communication Coach, is the catalyst behind building great teams for a growing list of private practices and companies. His specialties include strategic analysis, establishing and reinforcing core values, opening communication, and instilling discipline so your team can thrive while fulfilling your entrepreneurial vision.

Morgan was born to communicate with others and his role as a consultant and coach allows him the opportunity to challenge the status quo, seek continuous improvement within your organization, and improve the lives of entrepreneurs around the world.

Wise beyond his years and instinctually described as a 'strategist' by Kathy Kolbe, the world's leading authority on human instincts, Morgan continues to defy convention, challenge his coaching clients, and motivate entrepreneurs to build autonomous teams to more quickly realize their vision. His experience includes:

- Kolbe Certified Consultant

- Strategic Communication Coach to practices spanning the entire United States; from Hawaii to Alaska, and California to Massachusetts.

- Former Director of Operations for an Inc. 500/5000 Organization

- Led America's Highest Rated Hearing Health Care Team

- Leading Change Initiatives Based on the Disney Institute and Ritz Carlton Methods

- Innovative Teaching, Coaching and Leadership for Multiple Health Care Professions

FREE
RESOURCES

WhyTheyThrive.com/resources

TESTIMONIALS

"The follow-through and accountability that Morgan provides in a straight shooter method is exactly what I need at times. The flurry of running a business weighed on me without Morgan's voice of reason on the other end of the phone."

DR. LAURA VINOPAL
PROFESSIONAL HEARING CARE

"I've owned my audiology practice for over 20 years. Morgan has been instrumental in evaluating candidates to add to my staff who are the right fit for the role. Because of this, we have been able to change the entire culture at our office, and this change has added more productive and happy employees! I thank Morgan for changing my life and my business!"

DR. LARRY CARDANO
HEARING CENTER OF LONG ISLAND

"Morgan's ability to communicate the Kolbe System is incredible. He makes the complex so simple for me and my staff, and making sure that everyone on our team is in the right position to serve the business and each other has changed our organization. I can't thank Morgan enough as an advisor to our practice and for helping me with my team."

MIA MOUNTS
MODERN HEARING SOLUTIONS

LEARN WHAT OTHERS HAVE TO SAY AT
WhyTheyThrive.com/resources

SCHEDULE A
FREE 'WHY THEY THRIVE'
STRATEGY SESSION

TalkToMorgan.com